Life As I Know It

Life As I Know It

EMELINDA P. EASON

authorHOUSE®

AuthorHouse™
1663 Liberty Drive
Bloomington, IN 47403
www.authorhouse.com
Phone: 1-800-839-8640

First published by AuthorHouse   12/01/2011

ISBN: 978-1-4670-3480-7 (sc)
ISBN: 978-1-4670-3481-4 (ebk)

Library of Congress Control Number: 2011916275

Printed in the United States of America

PERSONAL STATEMENT

I have wanted to write a book about my life and stages of my life where I was born, my descendants, how I have lived and how everything around me has affected my life differently.

My life as I know it from small child living on the Island continues on to a place where I will spend the rest of my life.

This book is dedicated to my love ones, my husband, my children and my grandchildren, and their children's children. I want them to know where I came from, my other side of the family.

INTRODUCTION

*I*n able to know who I am I want to start writing from the beginning of my life. I was born on the month of November, Thanksgiving Day, on the Island of Philippines in Cavite City. Outskirts of Manila and it is its own city with high walls and iron gates.

We lived with my grandparents and I rarely see my dad because he was in the United States Navy and he goes overseas a lot. When he does come home, I remember he would have with him lots of surprises for my brother and I. As a child I would always enjoy those moments having my dad home. I remember he had brought me a beautiful walking doll, and for my brother he had brought him a playing guitar. My brother and I felt like he was a stranger, we couldn't ever get close to him, even though he's our dad.

I was closed to my grandfather; he has always been there for me when I was a child. I remember he would tell us his childhood stories and the time when his father came to the Island. He would also tell us about my grandmother and how they have met each other and during the time of World War II when Japanese invaded the Philippine Island. My cousins and I would sit on the floor listening while he tells us about his life.

MY FAMILY LINE

*M*y grandfather whom I call papa is half Spanish and half Filipino. His father, my great-grandfather was born in Madrid, Spain. He had one brother and they both went their separate ways. My great-grandfather joined the Spanish army and his brother decided to go to Mexico.

During the Spanish and Philippine war my great-grandfather married my great-grandmother, a Filipino girl from Pampanga Province. After the civil war my great-grandfather and my great-grandmother stayed on the island as their permanent home. He was a very ambitious man; he had purchased several lands around the islands. He was in the business of buying and selling properties.

When my great-grandfather had passed away, he had it in his will to divide his assets between his children. My grandfather the youngest of five siblings left him the most of his assets including his business.

My grandfather married my grandmother; she is half English and half Chinese. My grandmother was a beautiful woman, she was tall and she had a smooth white complexion, she had a long beautiful hair.

My dad was half Portuguese and half Filipino. His father came from Portugal and married his mother a Filipino from Cebu. My dad grew up in a suburb of Cebu City; he came from a poor family. He saw an opportunity to join the United States Navy and made something of himself.

My dad gave us an opportunity for a new life in another country, and when we left the island and headed to America, I was sad that I had to leave the life I knew. I was leaving my grandparents, uncles, aunts, cousins and friends, the people I love and adored. I have had a good and happy childhood on the island, and now I am entering a new life in a country that is unknown to me.

MY LIFE AS A CHILD
ON THE ISLAND

Cavite City was a place where I lived as a young girl. We were living with my mom's parents, while my dad is over seas. The family name was well known throughout the island, they're well thought of and respected by the community and they called them Aristocrats; because of their family name. I remember friends would come by and visit my grandfather just to talk with him or asked for his advice.

The family owns several business, my grandfather's nephew was a Mayor of the community and his other nephew was a chief of police. His sister works for the American Embassy in Manila, and she was the person who prepared our passports.

I remember living in a big two story Spanish house with lots of rooms. The floor was maple wood, and all the windows was clear glass and beautiful Spanish doors. The veranda was exquisitely shaped with climbing vines. There were also different types of flowers complimenting the landscape of the veranda. I have always liked that place the most; it was my hiding place where I can be alone. The big house surrounded by palm trees and different kind of fruit trees.

My grandparent's had eleven children, one of the siblings passed away when he was born. We all lived in the big house; we had maidservants to take care of the house and a nanny to take care of us. We were very fortunate to live with my grandparents.

My cousins and I enjoyed playing outside, running around playing hide and seek, hop scotch, tossing coins and whatever games we can think of to play. I remember on the day it would rain we would go outside, we would dance in circles with our hands out to the sides, and we would have our mouths open to drink the rain. We were enjoying the moment until our mom has called us in to the house.

I remember when there was no school the whole family went to Manila to the market place, and to visit friends. I rode the scooter with my uncle, the fresh air touching my face and thinking; it's like riding on the wind. My first experienced riding on the scooter and I loved it, and I enjoyed every moment of that ride.

When we got to Manila, I wanted to ride the carriage, which a person pulls the carriage with all his might. I gave him money to take us to the market place which wasn't too far away; I just wanted to experience the ride. This is how some people make their living to survive.

We would walk to each vendor to buy meats, vegetables and fruits, and also other things they have to sell at the market place. After that we would stop at the restaurant and have lunch. I remember I would always order coca-cola to drink; I didn't care if I eat or not, I just wanted my coca-cola. We left the restaurant and headed back home and I rode back with my uncle.

Before dinner, my grandmamma went to the kitchen to help the maids prepare the meals. All the men went to the living room having they're usual conversations. My cousins and I are playing in the den, and we can hear our mother's playing cards in the other room.

My grandmother called everyone to the dinner table; it was set with beautiful china and silverware. The tall crystal glasses have been filled with water and the small glasses was filled with red wine, for this is the Spanish tradition. Our sitting arrangements are that grand-papa sitting at the head of the table and grandmamma sitting at the other end of the table. My uncles and their wives and my aunts and their husbands sitting opposites from each other with their children.

We have prayer before dinner, then we wait for grandfather's gesture that we can all start eating. But before we can consume our food, the maid went around with the bowl of water as we can wash our hands before we eat. We dried our hands with the cloth napkins and handed it to the maid. During dinner time we all converse with each other telling what we did that day, and we laugh at the silliest story.

I remember once a month after dinner, my grandpapa would open the gate for the mountain people to perform for us. They call themselves the "Moro People" because they lived on the mountains. They have beautiful costumes, and they would play their instruments that's made out of bamboo. The parent's and their children performing their theatrical dance. One particular dance they've perform is the tinkling, it's the art of Philippine dance with rhythm and speed. It was amazing to see how they can prevent from getting hurt and getting their feet caught between two bamboos.

My cousins, my brother and I were watching the whole events from upstairs window, and every time they would stop performing we would throw money down. When it was over my grandpapa had given them money for their service and thanked them for coming, then he closed the gate behind them. I have always enjoyed and look forward to this special occasion.

My cousins would call me tomboy because I like playing with trucks and I would climb trees with them, I wasn't afraid of anything. I remember playing with my cousin one day, we were playing with marbles on the ground and we would hit it with another marble with our thumbs and forefingers to see how many we could hit, and I would hit the most marbles.

I also remember my friends and I were playing and throwing coins against the concrete wall to see who can toss the coins on top of the other. The games we play as children was enjoyable and fun, and we have such an imagination.

One afternoon the whole family went to the beach and we would dig for clams for our clam bake. My cousins and I would make sand castles, and we would run around the beach barefooted. We stayed until it got dark and my uncles built a big bonfire, and we sat in circles holding hands, we would sing and then some of us would make jokes and telling stories. That night we enjoyed every moment in time with each other.

CATHOLIC SCHOOL

During my school year, I attend St. Joseph Catholic School. I remember I had to wear uniforms, white blouse with long sleeves, blue flannel skirt with ridges, a knee high white socks with white shoes, and a tie to wear with the uniform. Everything had to be clean and pressed and the white shoes had to be polished and shiny that I can see my reflection.

Before I went to school, my mom would brush my hair and part it to the side and she would put artificial flower on my head, I hated that hairdo, and when I leave the house I would take it off. I also remember she would experiment with my hair, she had given me a perm and it turned out so curly and I couldn't even brush it.

I have gotten my share of troubles in school with the nuns, they were very strict and they take everything serious and they seem that there is no humor in their life. One day in math class my friend and I were pulling a prank on the nun, I had put a banana under her seat cushion before class started. When she enter the class room she sat down in her seat and the banana got squashed, and everyone was laughing.

The Nun didn't have any idea what just happened, but she did noticed that the whole class was laughing. She got agitated and asked the class as to why we're laughing, we all got quiet and didn't say anything. The Nun got up from her chair to show the class a few math problems on the blackboard. When she got through, she went around her desk and lift up the chair cushion and found the squashed banana. She then realize that was why we're laughing about earlier. She got angry and ask the class who's responsible of placing the banana under her seat cushion, the whole class didn't say a word. Then she threatened the class if we didn't come forward with the truth she would call our parent's to the school.

I stood up and confess to the whole incident to the sister that it was my idea. The sister had that surprise look on her face that I acted alone, then she told me she's not please with me. Then she send me to Mother superior's office with the note. As I was walking down the hall I was afraid to see Mother Superior and all kinds of thoughts running through my mind.

When I was in Mother Superior's office I gave her the note, she open the note and read it. I watched her open her desk drawer and she took out a ruler, then she walk toward me and told me to hand out both of my hands in front of her, then she told me to steady my hands palms up, then she would hit my hands as hard as she could five times with the ruler, after that she told me to turn my hands over and to lower it down and she did the same way five times and my knuckles was hurting. All that time she was hitting me with the ruler I kept myself from crying even though I was in pain, I did not want her to see me crying.

When I left her office I went to the girl's bathroom and cried, I looked at my hands and it was so red and hot and I let the cold water run through my hands to soothe the redness and the pain in my hands. I stayed in the girl's bathroom in one of the stall waiting for the time to go home.

After school my uncle was waiting to take us home, I didn't say anything to anyone what had happened in school for I know that I will get into trouble again. I kept this incident a secret from my family, and the catholic school never inform my mom of the incident.

There was this other incident happened at school, I was disrupting the whole class by talking with the classmate. Then the Nun told me to go in the closet, so, I did and she locked the closet door. I sat in the dark until the sister open the door and told me to come out, my eyes were squinting trying to focus. I've noticed that the whole class was looking at me and everyone was so quiet and they looked at me with sadness in their eyes.

I have learned the ways of catholic school, the Nun's and their rules and regulations. They're the authority figure with strict rules, children are not allowed to question their authority and we are only to listen and obey them.

One day my cousin and I decided to walk home from school and we didn't get home until three hours later. When we got home everyone was angry with us and asking where we have been. I was trying to explain to them that we just wanted to walk home for a change. Then grandpapa enter the room with his strong firmed voice and told my mom and my aunt that he wanted to talk with us. They left the room without hesitation; and I'm thinking to myself "we are in trouble now."

We both bowed our heads down and kissed his right hand, this is a sign of respect to him. Then my cousin and I looked at each other with dismay. Grandpapa questioned us as to why we decided to walk home from school. My cousin replied that it was my idea to walk home, then I looked at her putting the blame on me. Then he excused my cousin so he can talk to me alone, I was kind of scared and uneasy to be alone with him, because I didn't know what to expect. Even though that my grandfather is a soft spoken man with a big heart and he never raise his voice with anyone, and yet I fear him. It's a kind of fear with respect and disappointment that I feel and knowing that I'm his favorite grandchild and somehow he's not please with me.

Grandpapa walk toward to his favorite chair and sat down, he paused for a moment then he motioned for me to sit on the floor before him. Then he started saying that everyone including him; they were concerned and worried, when my cousin and I didn't show up for dinner. Grandpapa did not yell or scolded me, instead he lectured me of the simple rules of life and responsibility. The wrong choices we make and the consequences that goes along with it. I loved my grandfather even more and truly respected him. In his eyes I couldn't do anything wrong, I felt bad and ashamed that I disappointed him.

MY FIRST COMMUNION & CONFIRMATION

*M*y first communion was memorable, remembering everyone was fussing over me. My godmother who is also my aunt made the dress for the occasion, it was white with long sleeves silk dress with the neckline of embroidered lace and the hem line was sewed with gold lace. And she also made a veil that goes with the dress with flowery headband.

When the time has come everyone was at the church waiting and anticipating for my arrival. When I entered the sanctuary; I saw how beautifully the church was decorated. The purple cloth around the altar, and on each side of the altar there was flowers of white lilies. The purple curtains complementing the picture of Jesus above the altar. These church was beautifully built with painted mosaic windows, and pictures of all the saint's around the room and ceilings.

During communion the Bishop performed his priestly duty and said a few verses from the bible, and when he got finished speaking, he motioned for me to walk toward the altar with my rosary in hand. Then I knelt down before him and then he placed his right hand on top of my head, speaking in Spanish and giving me his blessings.

After that I received the communion and then he sprinkled holy water on me.

After the communion we all went home to celebrate my special day. The maid prepared all kinds of food and set everything on the table. The bishop was there, my grandfather had invited him to celebrate with us. We all took our seats and before we can eat, my grandpapa asked the bishop if he can say grace.

I can see that everyone was having a good time, everybody was there except for my dad. After dinner I opened my presents, I had all kinds of gifts from everyone. I enjoyed that day it was wonderful and I was a happy little girl.

MY OTHER SIDE
OF THE FAMILY

I remember going to Cebu with my mom and my brother to visit my dad's family. We rode the bus to Manila and when we got there, we then had to ride the big boat called the "Flying Fish" to take us to Cebu. When we reached Cebu we rode another bus to take us to my grand-mother's place.

Cebu is one of many islands in the Philippines; and the people there speaks their own language. People on the streets were selling chickens, and I also noticed that there are some people have roosters, and they were letting their roosters fight each other.

When we got to my grandmother's house her daughter and her son opened the door, and they're both welcomed us to their house with hugs and kisses. This is the first time that I actually met my grand-mother and my dad's sister and brother. They also greeted my mom, then my aunt asked her if she brought any money with her from my dad. My mom opened her bag and pulled out a white envelope full of money, she then gave it to my aunt. All three of them were talking in a different language I couldn't understand, then I asked my mom what kind of language they're speaking, she then told me they are speaking in Visayan language.

We didn't stay very long at my grandmother's house, all that time my brother and I we're clinging to my mom, we both felt uneasy. My grandmother asked us to stay for dinner, but mom told her that she wanted to leave before it got dark. That was the last time I saw of them.

MOM AND DAD

*M*y dad came home from Japan and he had all kinds of gifts with him for everyone. I have noticed that my grandparents don't think highly of my dad, I supposed it's because of what had happened years before.

My mom had told me her story; how she met my dad, it all started back after World War II. My mom was nineteen and she was the fourth youngest of the girls. My dad he was in the United States Navy, he was on leave visiting his family.

My grandparents owns a restaurant, and they were very busy that day. My grandmamma called up to the house, to send my mom to help out. While my mom was working with the cash register, she noticed that my dad was looking at her. Then my dad asked my mom's sister if he could talk to her, and be his server.

My aunt gave her the message, she then walk to his table and took his orders, she didn't give him the opportunity to converse with her. My mom didn't want to serve him at all so she asked her sister to serve him.

That night when she was balancing the cash register and she was by herself, my dad's navy buddy was waiting for her to close the restaurant. While she was locking the door he came up to her and asked her if she wanted to buy boxes of carton of cigarettes for their store, and he would take her to the place where it was selling. She knew the person she was talking with and she trusted him, so she then went with him.

When she got to the place she saw my dad, she asked the man as to why he had brought her. He then replied that my dad just wanted to talk to her. She had fear in her eyes and she didn't know what to do, and she was thinking what her parent's would do if they found out what had happened.

It was getting late that night and my mom was afraid to go home, so my dad took her home with him to his family. Hours had passed and morning came, my grandmother noticed that my mom didn't come home that night. She got worried and told my grandpapa and he was furious, he then told his son's to go out to look for her. They have contacted every family members and friends if they have seen her, and nobody knows where she's at or what had happened.

Several weeks had gone by and there's still no report about my mom, until one day someone came forward and told my grandmamma where she was living. She went to my dad's mother's house to talk to my mom and to bring her home. While they were talking my grandmother gave her a choice to either stay with my dad or go home with her, my mom told her that she was afraid to face my grandpapa and that she also knows how she had disgraced the family name, and also told her that she loved my dad and she wanted to stay with him.

That night after family dinner and everyone was in the den, grandmamma was talking to grandpapa that she had found my mom and had a talk with her. She told him my mom's decision to stay with my dad, he got very angry and he instructed everyone not to mention of her name and that he himself disowned her.

Eight Months had gone by and my mom was pregnant with me, and my grandmother would visit her secretly, in spite of what my grandfather had said. On the week of my dad's schedule to leave to go overseas, mom and dad went to talk to my grandfather to reconcile with him. They both asked him for his forgiveness and told him that she's with child and she's going to need the support from her family. That day my grandfather forgave them and he embraced my mom and welcomed her back to the family; they're both had tears in their eyes. My mom was happy and knowing that her life is going to change forever, and she has the love and support from her family.

The day has arrived for my dad to go overseas, and my mom went back home to her family while he's gone, but she was also sad that he was going away for awhile. She was happy to be back with her family again and they all treated her like she had never left.

THE LETTER

$\mathcal{M}$om got a letter from dad telling her that the Navy is transferring him to California permanently, and that he had already arranged for us to move to California. When mom told my brother and me the news, we looked at each other with amazement. I started having knots at my stomach and thinking of going to a different country scares me. I did not want to leave my grandparents and all of my relatives and friends, and thinking that I will not be able to see them anymore.

My mother struggled with this decision; she did not want to leave her family. She was making something of herself, a business of her own; buying and selling furniture. She went to talk to her father for his advice, and to tell him that she did not want to leave her family. My grandfather told my mom "you have built your own family and you have you're own life, and where your husband go you must also go with him."

Looking back, we were very fortunate to live with my grandparents and the love we have for each other. The faith we have as a family that binds us together and having strong moral values. My life as a child taught me many things that life is full of challenges and not to forget where I come from.

It was the summer of 1959, I remember going once a week to get our shots and vaccinations at the United States Embassy in Manila for our trip to America, and taking pictures for our passports.

When the time came for us to leave the island everyone was there to bid us farewell, everyone was sad, and yet they are happy for us. I looked at my grandpapa with tears in my eyes and I can see the sadness on his face. We embraced each other and I was crying and I did not want to let go, then he said to me "go with God and I love you and I will miss you." That was the saddest moment of my life.

VOYAGE TO AMERICA

*A*s the ship slowly leaving the port and we still waving good-bye is to our loved ones, and as it rolls further and further out to the sea, they all seemed so small and disappeared in an instant. I remember it was a warm day when we left Philippine Island. I was watching the ocean water beating against the side of the ship, and then I looked up and realized that I cannot see the island anymore.

I stood there for a while mesmerized by this huge ship that I am standing on, then I heard my mom's voice and she is motioning me to go with her and we took the elevator to second floor to our cabin. As we entered the room it was a two bedroom with a living space, one window and I can see out to the ocean, and it has a bathroom.

After we had settled in, my brother and I went exploring; we found the theater, and we sat down to watch cartoon until it was over. Then we went back to our cabin; mom was waiting for us, so that we can go to have lunch. We all went down to the dining room and the waiter lead us to our table. I have noticed that all the tables were decorated with flowers as centerpiece, and name cards was placed on the table for seating arrangements. And we had another family sitting at the table with us.

After lunch, I went walking on the deck and stopping to look at the ocean while standing on a small bucket that I have found. That afternoon it was breezy and a little cool and I was staring at the horizon, it was beautiful and peaceful and I can even hear the ocean breeze.

I stood there for a while enjoying the moment and writing in my diary, then my brother tapped me on the shoulder telling me that mom was looking for me. We both went up to our cabin and my baby sister was playing on the floor with her toys. I then played with her, as I was looking at my sister and remembering the time when she won the baby contest for the most beautiful baby. I played with her for a while and then I went to lie down before dinner.

I remember that one particular night everyone was asleep, and then there was a knock on the door telling us that we need to go down to the deck as the captain requested. When we got to the deck everyone was there and all passengers was in panic. The captain announced that there has been a leak down in the basement and for all of us not to panic and to put on the life jackets for this was the standard procedures. I can see that everyone was frightened especially the children holding on to their parents for comfort.

It took them for hours to fix the problem and the night was long and cold. Then the captain came on the P. A. System announcing that the problem has been fixed and that we all can go back to our cabins. I will never forget that night, as a child I was afraid that something drastic could have happen.

Days had gone by after the incident. One morning after breakfast the ship was approaching the island of Guam, some passengers were standing on the deck and some are inside watching, everyone was getting excited and anticipating to see the small island. As the ship getting closer to the port, the captain announced that the ship will dock on the island of Guam for couple of days for maintenance and fuel, and we are all free to visit the island.

Mom told us that we are going to visit her brother for couple of days. We left the ship and took a taxi to my uncle's place of work. When we got there, my uncle was surprised and happy to see us, and then he had his friend take us to his house. When we arrived to his place, I was amazed and it took my breath away that he lives by the ocean and secluded, it was beautiful.

The next day he took us on a tour of the island and showed us the place where Magellan had landed on the island. Then he took us on the top of the mountain to show us a little cave where Magellan had rested, he told us the history of the island. Guam is a little island by itself and not much to see, but there are beaches around the island. After the tour, my uncle took us to meet his friends.

That evening my uncle has invited a few friends for dinner, they all seems to be having a good time especially my mom, she's happy and content. As for me, I stepped out for a little while enjoying the cool night breeze. I lied down on the hammock looking up at the night sky and gazing at the stars. I felt the cool ocean breeze and I was thinking how peaceful it is.

The next day we had to get ready to go back to the ship and my uncle took us back in his jeep. I looked at my mom she was so sad she had tears in her eyes. We said our good-bye's and embraced each other, it was hard for my mom to leave love one's behind.

We boarded the ship and as it rolls out of port everyone was still waving good-bye's to their love ones. We went down to our cabin to unpack our belongings and to relax for a while. I asked my mom "where's the ship going to now? she then replied, that it's going to Hawaii and from there we are to take the plane to California.

Morning came, we all woke up early to get ready for breakfast, we had to be in the dining room by 8:00 that morning. As the day progress my brother and I went to see a movie, I couldn't even remember what I was watching, my mind had wandered off. I was thinking of my grandpapa and how much I was homesick, wishing that I was back home and playing with my cousins. I missed listening to my grandpapa telling of his childhood stories, and how I missed my life back on the island. As a child I was happy and content and I feel secure with them. My grandparent's they have always been there for me, my mom she was always busy with her business and my dad he goes overseas a lot.

The voyage to America seems long, I suppose when you're at sea for so many days feelings of anxiousness sets in. I finally accepted that America will be my permanent home for the rest of my life. I was on the deck that night looking on the horizon and the moon was shining down at the water, it was beautiful and peaceful just being there on the open water. I know I was just a young girl, but I remember how it made an impression on me. I have learned about God's creation through catholic school, and seeing all these is amazing.

When we reached the Island of Hawaii we stayed several days with relatives, my mom's cousins. I remember going through the plantations and one of my cousin's went up on top of the coconut tree and chopped one of the coconut. Then he cracked it open and we drank the coconut milk, then he sliced a piece of coconut with his knife and gave me some to eat. After that, we cut a bark of sugar cane and we taste the juice, it was so good.

All day long my mom's cousins have been preparing for the luau for that night, I've been smelling the cooking of all kinds of food in the house and they've been roasting a whole pig over the fire. This celebration was for us, to wish us happiness and prosperity on our new life in California.

That night everyone was having a wonderful time dancing, eating and laughing with each other. Then they had Hawaiian dancers for entertainment and one of my cousin's sang the song and all that I can remember it was a beautiful song. We had luau all night long by the beach.

After staying three days with relatives they took us to Honolulu airport that late afternoon to catch the plane to California. That was the first time I ever rode the plane, they even served us a regular meal. When the plane was getting closer to the airport I can see all the bright lights below, it was exciting and fascinating at the same time.

CALIFORNIA MY NEW HOME

*W*e landed in San Francisco airport and we were waiting for my dad to pick us up. We was looking for him all through the crowds hoping that we'll soon see him. The waiting and the anticipation to see my dad was more of disappointment. Hours has passed, then my mom made a call to my dad again, but there's still no answer. Finally mom decided that we should get a hotel room to stay overnight. The night was cool as we're waiting for taxi to take us to the hotel, and when we got there, it was an old century Victorian on top of the hill.

When we got to our room, mom tried calling dad again, and still there's no answer. Then mom decided that we should go down to the dining room to have something to eat, and that she will try again tomorrow to call him. As we're waiting for our orders to come I've noticed on mom's face that she was worried and concerned that she couldn't get hold of my dad.

The following morning we all got up early to have breakfast. Then mom remembered that she had the red cross number my dad gave her in case she couldn't get in touch with him. After breakfast we all went back to the room, she made a call to red cross and talking to someone explaining her situation. Later that day red cross called her back and told her that they got hold of the Navy and that they will inform my dad that his family is in San Francisco. Red Cross also told mom that the ship he is on will be out to sea for two weeks.

We've enjoyed our stay in San Francisco and we went to Fishermen's Warf, we visited the museum and we rode the cable cars. As a child I was amazed how big a city San Francisco is with beautiful sceneries and landscapes. Alcatraz standing alone in the middle of the ocean, the Golden Gate Bridge is the most beautiful of all, of San Francisco. It was cool and windy that day when we're exploring the city and then we ate dinner at the Chinese restaurant in China Town.

After two weeks dad picked us up from the hotel, mom was happy to see him and we are all happy to see each other. Dad told us our home is to be in Alameda and we are living in the apartment his renting. When we got to the place it was a two story apartment house and we live upstairs. It was a three bedroom apartment with a small kitchenette, living room and one bathroom, and yet it was large enough for five people to live in it.

The town of Alameda; a small city by the shore and closed to Naval Base where my dad works. Downtown Alameda has old Victorian houses and lots of shops and places to eat, and also there is a Tunnel between Alameda and Oakland. Dad took us to his place of work at the Navy Exchange where he works as a barber. After that he took us to the ship he was on while he was out to sea for two weeks for training, he gave us a tour of U.S.S Midway, aircraft carrier.

We also spend our days visiting friends and going to places like Oakland and then going to Hayward, he had a good friend that lives there and he wanted us to meet him and his family. After that we ate dinner at his favorite Chinese restaurant, we had a good time that night as a family.

ELEMENTARY SCHOOL

On the month of September, dad enrolled my brother and I to Elementary School in Alameda, the school system held us back one grade because our education in a different country doesn't meet their school standard.

I felt so out of place I wanted to runaway, I didn't want my dad to leave us in the school with all these strangers. I can hear him saying "it will be alright and before you know it, you will be making friends." That morning my homeroom teacher took me to the class and the other teacher took my brother by his hand, and we both looked at each other walking in a different directions.

When I got to my class the teacher had an assigned seat for me at the far left of the room by the window. Then she asked me if I can speak English, I told her that I can, and also told her that catholic school I attended taught me how to speak English which is the main subject, and I also told her that I can speak Spanish fluently.

Going to public school is quite different compared to private school. In public school there is no uniform, I can wear any clothes I want that is appropriate to school standard, also students are free to roam in the class room. American school are more open, I can actually talk to the teacher when I'm having a problem. I have learned to adjust the American way of life and so far I like it.

One thing I've noticed in American Children they talk back to their parents and whined more to get what they want. I remember that day when a little boy wanted his mother to buy him a toy, he kept on and on, then finally she got agitated and spanked him and bought the toy. I found her action a little disturbing, spanking him in public. I thought to myself perhaps this is the way American parents discipline their children no matter where they are.

I made new friends at school and around my neighborhood. After school I went outside to play with my friends and we stayed out until it got dark.

MOM'S FRIEND

*W*hile we're living in Alameda mom made a friend, American lady who lives downstairs with her daughter and son, her husband is in the Navy and he's away a lot. Mom and her friend would visit each other every morning and having coffee, they became good friends.

One day she gave her daughter a birthday party outside on the front yard of the apartment and mom helped her with the party. Everyone was having a good time, I did noticed that dad did not like this lady and the friendship that mom and her have for each other.

The next day mom's friend invited her to the Tupperware Party and she was excited to go. That evening she had made dinner for us before she went to the party, and dad wasn't home yet from work. Dad got home late that night and asked where mom was, which he already knows because she told him that morning. I can tell by the look on his face that he's very upset about her going to the party.

Late that night dad and I was still up watching television and we heard mom unlocking the door, but dad got up to put the chain on the door. As she tries opening the door, dad told her she couldn't come in, mom pleaded with him to unchain the door. They would argued back and forth and dad would yell at her. I got up and told dad to open the door and to let her in, but he wouldn't. My brother and my little sister woke up, then he told me to take my brother and my sister back to the bedroom and for us to stay there. I can hear my mother crying outside the door and pleading with my dad. That night I was afraid of my dad, I couldn't do anything and I was nervous and my stomach was in the knot. I was afraid, my siblings and I we're crying for my mom.

Mom was cooking dinner and I've noticed that dad was making himself a drink. I asked him what he was drinking, but he never answer me. Lately dad would fix him a drink every night before dinner, most of the time he would drink beer. I have seen my mom struggle with this kind of life that she is not use to. Her family so far away from her not able to talk with them or visit. I can tell she feels lost without them, I can understand how she feels because I too, am lost.

We finally met all my dad's friends, his navy buddies, their wives and their children. We would go to their houses for parties every weekend, they would greet each other with words of compadre and comadre and as for us kids, they want us to call them aunt's and uncle's, out of respect for them. While they're having a party, all the kids would be in another room watching television or playing a game. Sometimes I don't look forward to their parties, I would rather stay at home.

DAD'S RETIREMENT

A year has gone by and on the month of June the school was out for the summer. We moved to Oakland, my dad retired from the Navy. He continued his employment at the Navy Exchange as a barber in Alameda Naval Base. We lived in a two-story house and we had a downstairs neighbor, they have two young kids in my age, I can play with.

It was hard for me to move leaving my old friends and making new friends all over again, and after getting used to one place. The upside of all these I still have my friends that I met through my dad's friends, their children, we became like family.

Dad's retirement gave him more time to spend with the family, he works five days a week and he is off the weekend. We went places during summer vacation; the family would go to Vallejo to the flea market. I like going to that place because I can find books that I like to read and especially National Geographic magazine. Then we would stop at the city park and have a picnic.

On the weekend, dad and mom would go to horse races in San Mateo; they would take us along with them. We would have a picnic on the lawn then after that they would go and play the horses, my siblings and I would play games and stayed where we at.

Before summer ended, dad had a plan to take mom to Las Vegas, because she has never been there. We stayed in the hotel room while mom and dad went to the casino. They were gone for hours and I was still up watching television and waiting for them to come home, then mom and dad walked in the room and I asked if they've won, then he said, mom likes to play the slot machines, she enjoyed it so much she got hooked on the game.

FALL SEASON

$\mathcal{I}$ enrolled at Washington Elementary in Oakland going to fourth grade. The school is diverse with different cultures; the teacher's are very friendly and helpful with their students. I liked everything about the school and I also liked my classes, and I made new friends that day.

I participated in school activities, I love to play baseball and basketball, and I also signed up for track to challenge myself if I have the ability to run fast enough. After school they had girls try-outs for track and I was running against this girl, The coach said "I was fairly good," but not as good as the other girl. I found out right there and then I am not cut out for track.

Going into fourth grade is quite different I have witnessed one student bullying another student and I have never seen that before in any other schools I have attended. He made fun of this boy wearing glasses and called him four eyes and a geek. Also they make fun of underprivileged kids. I sometimes wonder about those kids who does the bullying, thinking maybe they have had an unpleasant home environment or they don't get the attention they need.

On the month of November dad took us to Reno, Nevada for the weekend. On our way there dad had a flat tire, so we stopped for awhile for him to change the flat tire. While he was changing the tire my siblings and I were playing on the snow throwing snow balls at each other, then we got the sled out of the trunk and we sled downhill.

After he finished putting a new tire on the car he wrapped the chains around the tire and we're back on the road again. When we reached our destination we checked in a motel, after that we went to the casino. While my parent's gambling, my brother and sister and I we're exploring each isles. Mom was playing the slot machines, and dad he was playing black jack, his favorite game to play. I remember he taught me how to play black jack and we would play it all the time.

We stayed in Reno until Sunday, that morning we stopped to have breakfast before we headed back home. It was snowing when we left, but the roads were clear and we didn't have any problem going home. It was a very long trip going back home, but we had a wonderful time together.

SAN LEANDRO

*W*e had lived in Oakland for three years, then we moved to San Leandro, California. My parent's bought a house which it would be home for us permanently. I was happy that we do not have to move again, I can actually say that this is home. It was a single family home with three bedrooms and one bathroom. It had a kitchen, a dining room with double door that opens to the patio, and a living room. We had a two car garage with the side door and a privacy fence all the way around the house. The property had a front and back yard with built in sprinkler.

San Leandro is a nice little town quite and pleasant, we lived close to the school and the grocery store is just a walking distance. When we finally settled in to our new home and meeting new neighbors, I remember an older lady who lives by herself our next door neighbor, she was friendly and kind. I would go to her house for a visit and she would always make me hot chocolate and she would have some kind of dessert that she made that day.

Now that we all got used to living in America, we're officially American kids. We talk and act like American kids as told by my dad when he's angry with us. Mom and dad they grew up in a different environment, their culture where there is strict discipline. So they discipline us like the way their parents disciplined them, I remember mom always told me that. As the years went by I have noticed that mom is more lenient with us.

I remember on November 22nd 1963, the day before my birthday. I was in the living room putting my make-up on getting ready to meet friends at the mall, and I was listening to the television, then I heard John F. Kennedy was assassinated in Dallas, Texas in the motor car with his wife. My heart sank and I started to cry, that day I forgot about the mall.

I remember the day when all schools were closed for his funeral we watched it on television, everyone was in mourning. I've heard people say that we have lost a good president.

On the year of 1964, the Beatles came to America. All the girls in school couldn't wait to watch them on television, they're schedule to perform on Ed Sullivan show. Mom bought me Beatles handbag and a big poster that I hung in my bedroom wall. I bought their record album and when my friends comes over to the house we would listen to their songs and sing along with them, those were the best of times.

LIFE CHANGING

*I*t was the summer of 1966, we went on vacation to Las Vegas, Nevada. We stayed at Caesar's Palace, and that night we went to see all the shows with mom and dad. During the summer, mom and dad took us for a four day trip to Disney Land, and also to the beach in San Diego. I remember going to Tijuana Mexico, we rode the buggy and bought Mexican pottery. I remember those times when we have family get together and we have so much fun as a family.

On September, I enrolled at Junior High School going into 7th grade, my brother and sister we're going to the Elementary School close to our house. Dad was working at the Moffett Field Naval Base as a Barber, and mom's pregnant at the time and she's due in October.

Our lives has change and dad has changed a lot as he became an alcoholic. I have seen him drink everyday when he comes home from work he drinks a can of beer or two, Then he would fix him a mix drink with vodka and water. I would wonder sometime why he drinks so much, but I never ask him that question, I suppose I was scared to ask.

When mom and dad would have a pleasant conversation, then all of a sudden it would turn into a big argument. I'd be angry with them that I get too nervous and I have a knot in my stomach. I couldn't bear hearing their argument and when dad drinks he doesn't know when to quit. They would argued back and forth to each other and blowing everything out of proportion, yelling at each other until he had enough and he would hit her, this is not the first time nor the last.

Growing up in the house I have always feared that every time my dad would drink and get drunk he thinks that he has to pick a fight with mom, and Little things he says that doesn't even amount to anything or worth fighting. I sometimes think he is so inclined of arguing with her that this is a normal behavior for him. I also wonder if they ever loved each other, I never hear them say "I love you" to each other.

On the month of October, my baby sister was born, that was the joyous moments of our lives. When mom brought her home she was so beautiful and tiny. I help mom take care of my baby sister especially at night when she wanted her bottle. I was the oldest of my three siblings and I have responsibility. When my baby sister was a month old she was christened at the Catholic Church. The two good friends of my parents became the godfather and the godmother. We had a big celebration afterwards and the party went on until midnight.

Many days had gone by without my parents fighting until one evening, they were arguing in their bedroom yelling at each other. I heard mom crying and I rushed in to their room and dad was out of control, hitting her repeatedly. I called one of his friends to come over to help us and explaining to him what was happening. Dad was already gone when he got to our house, he was talking to mom and he was suggesting that we should go with him to his place until things cools down. We stayed a few days with him and his family. I heard that dad was looking for us and one of his friend's told him where we were, then he came to take us back home.

Days and months had gone by and everything was back to normal and living like nothing has happened. I believe my dad is a good person, he just let alcoholism control him. Our lives is not always bad, we have some good times too, dad works hard and he provides for us. Dad has always made sure that we have family times, on spring break he would take us to Reno, Nevada and in the summer we would go to the park and have a family picnic. All summer long we always have somewhere to go. I remember the Navy would plan a big picnic for the military family on 4th of July every summer.

FRESHMAN YEAR

*A*fter two years of junior high, I graduated and looking forward of going to high school. In the year of 1968, I enrolled at Marina High School, my first year as a freshman. I liked all my classes, especially History and American Literature, these are my favorite classes. I also signed up for Political Science for extra credit.

After all the students were enrolled we was instructed to gather in the gym. The principal divided us into four groups of freshmen's, sophomore's, junior's, and senior's. Marina High is a four year school and we are the fighting Titans. We were having an assembly in the gym that morning, the Senior's and the Student Body welcomed all the Freshmen's to the school.

I was impressed of all the Senior's how friendly and helpful they were, I knew right there and then that I was going to like this school.

After the assembly we were instructed to go to our homeroom class. I have seven classes and I was looking forward to meet all my teacher's. My first class was American Literature, I've noticed the classroom was small and has seven desk. The teacher gave us a book to read "The Old Man And The Sea" that was our homework to do.

The following morning we are all in the Lecture Hall listening to the teacher and taking notes. Then he showed us the movie "The Old

Man And The Sea". The next day we have a group discussion in our homeroom class about the book. I enjoy going to these classes and I like interacting with my other classmates.

After school my friend's and I would meet outside the front lawn of the school and we would go to Taste Freeze for a couple of hours before we go home. Taste Freeze is the gathering place for all teenager's after school, we have so much fun when we're all together. Sometimes we would go to the Mall just to hang out and meet other people.

I have three best friends and we're unseperable, the four of us we do things together and we go to each other's house, we were like sister's. When we're not together we talk on the phone for hours. We tell all our secrets to each other, we cry and laugh together, and we have a bond that no one can break. No matter where we are or where life takes us we will always have each other.

Football season has arrived and every Friday morning all students are to meet in the gym for the pep rally. We we're divided by class: Freshmen's, Sophomore's, Junior's, and Seniors, we would have a calling contest for the loudest class, and the freshmen's won the contest and they presented us with the trophy. That night at the football game I met this guy and he's a senior from another school, he became my very good friend.

After he graduated from high school he was drafted to go to Vietnam war, I was with him when he left for San Diego for training. My heart sank out of fear that I probably will not see him again. While he was in Vietnam we would write to each other everyday and I would get his letters every other day. Then days and months has passed by and I'm not getting any more letters from him and the feeling of sadness came over me.

I hear a lot of controversy about the Vietnam war, because of the protesting in Berkley and in San Francisco. My best friend's and I went to San Francisco to join the protest to bring our soldier's home. The Vietnam war was a misunderstood war of all, the percentage of American people didn't understand the war.

Some are protesting against our soldiers and they even have signs saying "baby killers", they hear what they want to hear from the media without questioning as to why that happened. They didn't understand that those children were being used by the Vietcong armies. They strapped those children with grenades and telling them to get close to the American soldiers, that is cruel using innocent children.

In my freshman year my parents bought a restaurant in Oakland, California in the vicinity of all major businesses. Dad wasn't agreeable with the idea of having a restaurant, but he went along with it. Mom convinced him that it's a good investment. Mom worked hard at the restaurant, she would open early in the morning and she would get home late at night. Dad would help at times when he gets off from work, and my brother and I would help over the weekends.

As times went by, the restaurant flourish and her customer base increased. She had to hire another person to help her cook in the kitchen, she also hired a waitress, the daughter of her friend, and she had another cook on the grill. Mom was happy of what she had accomplished.

SOPHOMORE YEAR

On July 20th 1969, that was the summer when Apollo II went up to the moon, we were all sitting in the living room our eyes were glued on the black and white television and we're waiting and anticipating for that moment to happen. Then the space shuttle Apollo went up and as we watched it go up it was amazing. It was worth waiting for and history was made that day.

Freshman year has come and gone and it was a very good year for me and now I'm a sophomore and a year older, I am more comfortable and familiar with my surroundings. Marina High has welcomed a group of new freshman's in school. I was elected by the student body to be the big sister for the two freshman girls to show them around campus, that day we became good friends.

My brother also entered his first year of high school, he was excited to be a freshman at Marina High. During his freshman year there was this boy; a school bully, who has always picked on him because of his height. One day he got enough of it and struck the boy with his fist on the face, he got in trouble with the school and they suspended him for two days.

Once my dad found out what had happened at school, he was furious with my brother, and he was trying to explain to him, but dad wouldn't listen. So, mom pleaded with him not to do anything irrational, but dad wouldn't listen to her, then he told my brother to go to his room. I stopped my dad from going to my brother's room and told him "that it wasn't his fault and the boy was asking for it" then I further told him that the boy was the school bully.

Mom and I can hear the whip of the belt and we were crying and I can also hear my brother crying. That night dad went out and we're all sitting in the living room watching television, and my brother stayed in his room. I sometimes think that my dad has a split personality; one side of him is loving, playful and fun to be around with when he's not drinking, and when he drinks he is a completely different person when he's angry, then he becomes mean and hateful, I can see it in his eyes. I love my dad, I just don't like what he becomes when he drinks.

Marina High was offering driver's education course for extra credit and I took the course for six weeks. After six weeks I took the written test and I passed it and I had my driving permit. I was anxious to drive my dad's car, then I've noticed that he left the Malibu in the garage and I was tempted to drive it, then I told my sister's that we're going for a drive around the block. When I was driving the car; I felt so independent, so happy, but when we got home I couldn't park the car in the garage, I was having trouble parking it straight. I left the car on the carport and called my dad's friend for help, who happens to live just a block away from our house. He came, shook his head and he had a grin on his face, he got into the car and parked it in the garage.

That night my dad got home from work and I wanted to tell him what had happened and I just couldn't. While we're at the dinner table and talking to each other, I felt so guilty and I wanted to tell him then, but I couldn't find the courage to do it.

The next day after school I came home and my dad was already home, then he called me into his room and asked me if I had driven his car. I apologized to him for taking the car out of the garage without his knowledge. I thought he was going to yell at me, but he didn't. I was even prepared for him to ground me, but he didn't. I asked him how he found out, then he told me from his friend, and he also thought that it was hilarious. Dad made it plain to me that day not to take his car without his permission. And I also noticed that my dad wasn't drinking that day and he was thinking clearly and he was very understanding.

OLD MEMORIES

I remember the good times we've had as father and daughter and we would laugh a lot. He would teach me and my brother how to play poker and blackjack, and he would also play different games with us. He would teach me how to slow dance and I would place my feet on top of his and we would dance in our living room, he would say to me "dancing is art and to let my body move to the rhythm of the music".

Dad loves to play his guitar when he gets a chance and one night we were outside by ourselves and I would watch him play and listen to him sing, I sensed when he plays it gives him comfort. Then he looked at me and he said "I have high hopes for you". That night he talked about himself how he grew up in a poor family, and when he was a teenager, his dad would beat him with the belt for no apparent reason. He was 19 years old when he left home and he worked on several odd jobs just to survive.

In the year 1945, after world war II, he decided to stay in the U.S. Navy, he was 23 years old. He told me that gave him the opportunity to make something of his life. Then I looked at him with sad face and tears in my eyes, and that night I understood him.

I remember him taking me fishing by the bay in San Francisco, it was cold and windy. I really didn't want to go fishing and it's not my favorite thing to do, but I went jut to please my dad. He would put the bait on my fishing pole, because I wouldn't touch the worms and I would tell him, it's disgusting, then he would have a smile on his face. We stayed half a day fishing and we didn't catch any at all. We did enjoy each other's company and dad gave me a new meaning of togetherness as father and daughter.

SIXTEEN

I turned sixteen and I couldn't wait until I got my driver's license, dad took me to the Department of Motor Vehicle to take the road test. While I was waiting for the instructor, there's also another person waiting to take his road test. As we're talking and getting to know each other, the instructor walked up to us and introduced himself. Then he led us outside to the vehicle we are to use for the road test, then he told me to drive first and to take the Interstate toward Oakland. While I was driving on the Interstate he instructed me to change lane and to exit on the right toward downtown Oakland.

When I got to downtown Oakland, he then instructed me to turn in the least busy street, I turned to the right where there is hardly no traffic. Then he told me to stop the car and to put it in reverse to drive it straight back, and after that he wanted me to parallel park the car. Then he told the other person to get behind the wheel and to do the same thing I did and to bring us back to the Motor Vehicle Department. I was so glad that was over with for me.

When we got back to the Motor Vehicle Department the instructor gave me my papers and he told me to get my driver's license. I was very happy that day that I have passed my road test, and I was officially legal to drive in the State of California.

My dad was happy for me and when we got home I told my mom and my siblings that I got my drive's license. Then my brother commented that "he can't wait until he gets his driver's license also". Dad suggested that we should go out to eat to celebrate, that night we went to our favorite place the Chinese restaurant.

Friday morning, dad let me drive his Malibu to school and I picked up my two best friends and they're both happy for me. After school we went to Taste Freeze to hang out for couple of hours with our friends and connecting with each other and just having fun.

On Friday night my weekend to stay out late with my friends until midnight. We all gathered together at the Boulevard, we call it the drag strip, and we cruised around the Boulevard for hours. Then I met this guy from other school and he was a senior, and then we went to the Mexican Restaurant. We talked for hours just getting to know each other and then I invited him to my sixteenth birthday party, then I gave him the direction to my house, and after that we all left the restaurant and went back cruising the strip again.

On Saturday morning mom and dad was preparing everything for my birthday party. Dad was cleaning out the garage and placing tables and chairs, and mom was putting up decorations. They have turned the garage into a party room with balloons, and decorative party lights, and on the porch they have put up Chinese lanterns, the whole settings was beautiful.

That night everyone arrived at the party and they're mingling with other guest's and conversing with each other, some are eating and dancing to the music. My brother was the D.J. that night and he played all kinds of music from hard rock to Motown, I can see everyone was enjoying the party.

There were still some friends arriving at the party and one of them is the guy I met at the Boulevard that Friday night and he brought a friend with him, I must admit that I was surprised, I really didn't expect him to come to the party. I walked toward him, he then handed me a gift with a smile on his face and wished me a happy birthday, I, then thanked him for the gift and he can tell that I was happy to see him. Santana was playing and my Filipino friends were dancing to the cha-cha, and my school friends was watching them dance. I did noticed that they wanted to get on the floor to dance, but they didn't know how to dance the cha-cha, so my guy friend and I joined in and motioned to my school friends to join us also. That was the night they've all learned how to dance the cha-cha.

As the party progressing along and everyone was having a great time, my guy friend and I slipped outside for a moment. We talked about school and that he's the captain of the football team, and he also mentioned that he got a football scholarship to University of Southern California, he then concluded that his parent's wanted to meet me. I went back inside and told my brother that I'll be gone for awhile with my friend to meet his parents.

While we're there my dad showed up unexpectedly along with my friend's friend. He was very angry and told my friend not to even see me at all, and then he looked at me saying "he forbid me not to see him again." He grabbed my arm and he lead me to the car, we did not say a word to each other going home.

I was upset with my dad and embarrassed the way he conduct himself in front of my friend and his parents, the way he treated them, that was unacceptable. I couldn't even look at my dad and let alone speak to him, I was humiliated by him. I probably would not forget that night on my sixteenth birthday.

When I got home the party was still in full swing and everyone was still enjoying the night. Mom brought out the cake and it was beautiful, a two layered chocolate cake and it says "Sweet Sixteen", that night I pretended to have fun, but the memory of one bad situation stayed on my mind. The party ended at midnight and everyone was saying that they had a good time. My three best friends stayed over night to help me clean up.

That night I couldn't sleep it was still bothering me, I got up and turned the lights on and woke up my friends, and then told them what had happened. They were shocked and couldn't believe that my dad behaved like he did. We stayed up talking until morning, we were expressing our thoughts and feelings to each other and we discover that we share a common bond together.

JUNIOR YEAR

$\mathcal{M}$y Junior Year, and first day of school, I was glad to see all my friends. They were talking about what they did during the summer vacation; some actually went on vacation and other's stayed at home or worked during the summer break. During the summer break my friends and I went to the beach in Malibu, we met some guy's and we exchanged phone numbers.

My family and I went to Las Vegas for vacation, this is mom and dad's favorite place to go, and we stayed a week in Vegas. I also volunteered at the local hospital as a candy striper, and I loved working at the pediatrics department.

After fourth period it was lunch time, my friends and I placed our orders at the concession stand and we decided to eat outside on the lawn. I, happened to look up and I've noticed a girl and her two friends were making fun of a disabled girl and laughing at her, she was having difficulty getting away from them, because they had her surrounded. I told my friends what was going on; and so, I walked over there to tell the girl and her friends that they have no right to make fun of her. They told me to mind my own business, I, then told them; I'm making it my business, we exchanged words and the other girl came up to my face and I, then pushed her, she was about to hit me; then the bell rang.

Between classes I had to stop at the girl's restroom and it was full of smoke and it smells. Then I saw this girl, the one I had confrontation with, she was putting a lipstick on and she pretended that she didn't see me. I asked her; why she was mean to the girl, then she told me to shut-up and it wasn't any of my business. I looked at her with disgust, then a teacher walked in and told us to go back to class.

I was in my 7th period class and then the bell rang, I was headed to my locker and then my friend stopped me, she then told me what she had heard and everyone was talking about it, the rumor was that me and this girl was to have a fight after school.

When me and my friends were walking toward to my car, then I heard this girl calling me names. Everyone on the parking lot heard it and saying there's going to be a fight. I, then turned around and walked toward her, I was filled with anger, I looked at her and told her to repeat what she had said. She then pointed her finger to my face and I slapped it away, she then swung her right hand to hit me and then I ducked. I, then hit her on the face with my right hand, and then she grabbed hold of my hair and pulled me down on the ground. We we're soon hitting at each other, and I can hear the crowd yelling. When I finally got her pinned down, I was hitting on her left to right and I soon realized that I was hitting on her face. Then her two friends came to rescue her and hitting on my back and they were trying to pull me away from her. The next thing I knew my friends came to join in and everything broke loose. One of my friend's was wearing a big ring on her finger and she hit one of the girl with it and broke her nose and she was bleeding.

The girl's dean of school came out and broke the fight and took us into her office. After talking with us, she looked up at me saying "she had never expected this kind of behavior from me", then she suspended us for a week. When I got home that day from school, I told my parents what had happened and that I got suspended for a week. They're both upset with me and grounded me from driving the car and not having friends over at the house. I made use of my time while I was at home listening to music and I love to read a good novel, and I can still talk to my friends on the phone.

After a week suspension I was back in school and I was happy to see all my friends again, and they were all happy to see me also. I was in my 3rd class home economics and the girl I fought with approached me and apologized, after that we became friends. She started to hang out with me and my friends in school and after school, and she became part of our gangs. Her circle of friends didn't much want anything to do with her since she started hanging out with us.

Friday night we went to the football game, our usual night out, to cheer for our football team. After the game we stopped and ate, then we cruised the boulevard until midnight. Three of my best friends stayed over the night with me and we were talking about the school dance on Saturday night, and we talked for hours about anything and everything and it was getting late so we decided to call it a night.

Saturday night school dance and the gym was decorated beautifully with party lights and streamers and there was a lot of food. There were four teachers and parents to supervise our school dance. I over heard one of the teacher's talking to a couple of teenager's by the food table telling them that they have to leave the dance because they're behavior was unacceptable. The D. J. played K.C. and the Sunshine band and everyone was on the dance floor, we were line dancing to the music of "That's the way I like it". After the dance my friends and I decided to go to Jack London Square in Oakland to the teen club down under, it is one of our favorite places to go.

SPRING BREAK

All the juniors was to meet at the Half Moon Bay Beach, for the luau and a fun filled day with the Junior class. The beach was full of surfer and they're waiting on that big wave to come. It was a warm day at the beach, the sun was out and everyone was enjoying each other's company, some were playing volleyball and others were watching the surfer. Most of the Juniors stayed while it got dark and we build a bonfire and we danced to the music. The night was crisp and cool and we're enjoying the night at the beach.

The night was getting late so we left, I spend the night with my best friend Dee along with two of my other best friends Tina and Ela. The next day we had plans to go to Alameda and to San Francisco. We went to downtown Alameda and we shopped every store that is open, trying on clothes and shoes. Then we went to the music store and bought some LP's and 45's.

After shopping we decided to go to the beach where Clint Eastwood was staying in one of the apartments, we were hoping to see him, but we never did. After that we went to Alameda Naval Base to go bowling for a couple of hours, then on to San Francisco.

While we're bowling there was this guy, he was tall and well built, he had blonde hair, and he kept looking at me and smiling, then he finally had the courage to come forward and introduced himself and his friends to us. Then we asked them if they wanted to play one game with us and who ever loose will pay for dinner. My friends and I played competitively and they're not as bad either, but they lost and they took us to dinner at the Fisherman's Warf in San Francisco.

After dinner we walked the streets of San Francisco and as we're walking we stopped at the museum, after that we rode the cable cars toward china town. It was getting late that night, my friends and I we're ready to head back home, then he asked me for my phone number, I wrote it down in a piece of paper and handed it to him.

We started seeing each other every weekend and we would meet at samba's restaurant in Alameda. Then afterward we would go for a ride with his Harley Davidson along the coast of San Francisco. We got to know each other and enjoying each other's company, even though he's four years older than me. He had this bad boy image about him and I was attracted to him, and he's always been a perfect gentleman.

I remember the day he asked me to be his girl, we were in Santa Cruz on the beach by the board walk. It was kind of windy and a little cool and we're sitting on the sand watching the children fly their kites, then he gave me his high school ring with the chain and then he put it on my neck. We Stayed in Santa Cruz all day at the boardwalk and we rode the rides and played some games. After that, before midnight he took me home and when I got home mom and dad was still up watching television, and I sat with them awhile before I went to my room.

On the day of my dad's birthday he was working at the barber shop, R. W. and I stopped for a moment before we went to the Navy Exchange, so that he can meet my dad, they exchanged greetings and shook hands. I can tell that he was a little nervous meeting my dad, but he handled himself very well.

For the first time I did not want to go back to school, I didn't want spring break to be over. I wanted to spend more time and every moment of the day with R.W., our affection for each other has grown more and more each day and we couldn't wait to see each other, and when we're not together we talked on the phone for hours. He is the first guy that I actually got serious with, he was different from any guy that I have ever met.

LAST SEMESTER

$\mathcal{S}$pring break was officially over and everyone was back at school, the school hall was filled with students and teachers once more, and they all seemed happy to be back at school

My friends noticed that there was something different about me, then they perceived to tell me that I was neglecting them through spring break. I finally told them that I was seeing R.W. whom we have met at the bowling alley along with his friends, they remembered that day and Dee made a comment that she knew R.W. and I would be a couple.

The 3rd period bell rang and we went to our physical education class to get ready for our dance practice. We were at the girl's locker room changing in to our uniforms and talking, then Dee perceived to say that I should be careful about RW., and she also commented that she heard a lot about navy men and their reputation.

As we're walking in the gym I asked Dee, how she knows so much. Then the Instructor intervene and looked at us saying that "we're late" and then she instructed us to form a circle. Then she played the song "Aquarius" by the Fifth Dimension, and then we started to dance to the music. We were rehearsing for our upcoming musical event.

Friday finally arrived, RW picked me up after school on his Harley and dropped me off at Dee's house, and while he was waiting, Dee took me home so I can pick up a few things. I told my parents that I was spending the weekend with Dee. And as I was packing a few clothes, dad entered my bedroom and asked us what our plans for the weekend. Dee and I looked at each other and I said "we might go to the beach". I hated lying to my dad and yet I feel that I had to, because I know he will not approve of me seeing a navy guy and he's white.

When we got to Dee's house RW and I got on his Harley and we're headed to his sister's house for dinner. After that we went on to Santa Cruz, that night we went to the board walk and we rode the rides and played a few games. We stayed a few more hours and then on to San Francisco, after that he took me to Alameda Naval Base to show me his ship the "U.S.S Kitty Hawk" he told me about himself and what he does for the Navy. Then he told me that he's an officer, a lieutenant and he fly's the jet for the navy, and he also explained to me that sometimes I may not hear from him because of a mission.

That night when he took me back to Dee's house and we stayed a few minutes outside just talking, then we kissed and said our goodbyes for that night and looking forward for tomorrow. I couldn't sleep that night, I was so restless and I had so many things going through my mind. One thing I know was that I have fallen for him.

JUNIOR PROM

The night of the Junior Prom, Dee, Tina, Ella and I we're getting ready for our Junior Prom before our boyfriend's pick us up. We were helping each other out and then all of a sudden Dee's mother knocked on the door to let us know that our escorts has arrived. The four of us we're running around the room and we're not even close of being ready, so Dee told her mom to entertain the guys.

When we were coming down from upstairs Anne's mom were showing the guys pictures of their vacations. As we were leaving Anne's mom stopped us for awhile and said she "wanted to take pictures of us". We left the house that night and headed to San Francisco for our dinner reservation. We were to meet two other friends at the sea food restaurant.

We arrived at the prom and we took pictures, then we went on to our table. We're sitting at the table and watching everybody dance, then RW took my hand and lead me to the dance floor, and we slow dance. I sensed that night that he felt a little uncomfortable, so I asked him if he wanted to leave.

We left the prom that night and he took me to San Francisco, and when we got there, we walked toward Fisherman's Warf holding each other's hands. He was very quiet and I can tell that something was bothering him. We went down to the beach and sat on the sand and watching the ocean waves, and it was a little cool that night.

I was waiting for him to tell me what was on his mind, then he put his arms around me and he looked at me with a smile, and then I said "what" with a smile, then we kissed, and then he said "I'm falling in love with you. I was still waiting for him to tell me what's been bothering him all night. Finally, he told me that he got his orders to go overseas, my heart sank and I was silence for a moment, then I asked him "when" then he said "anytime". So, we sat there in silence holding each other tight, and tears were running down my cheeks. I wanted to tell him also that I love him too, but I didn't.

I remember the day he called me and asked me to meet him at the pier in Alameda Naval Base, but I didn't go, it hurts too much already and I knew in my heart that I will not ever see him again.

SUMMER OF 1970

$\mathcal{S}$chool was out for the summer and I had applied for a summer job at Blue Cross—Blue Shield of Oakland for a part-time job. I was working nights in the Insurance department sorting insurance claims and filing. I enjoyed working and making my own money and also it keeps me busy. I remember on my first pay check I opened up a savings account at the Bank of America in my name and I was proud of myself. From then on half of my pay goes to my savings and the other half I spend as I please, it's actually satisfying and I feel independent.

One thing I love to spend my money is on clothes and shoes, and I also love buying new record albums. On weekends when I'm not working my best friends and I would go shopping all day at Macy's, we love to go to the Mall just to hang out. I kept myself busy during the summer months doing volunteer work at Keiser Hospital and I loved helping people.

During the summer vacation my friends and I joined the theatrical Arts and Sciences in San Jose every afternoon, five days a week for four hours and it was only for three weeks, and we helped in the wardrobe department. We have enjoyed the whole acting crew and we made some friends along the way, and it was a learning experience for us.

One evening my friends and I went on a date to see the play of Romeo and Juliet in San Francisco. The theater was packed and our sits was up at the balcony. During the play we heard couple of guys behind us laughing at the scene when Romeo killed himself, we turned around and looked at them with disgust and told them that "they're very immature". After the play everyone stood up clapping and yelling to the word "bravo" and it was a long standing ovation.

Summer was almost over, so, my friends and I decided to go to Disney Land for the last time to enjoy our last summer season before we go back to school. When I got home from Disney Land I have noticed a pile of letters addressed to me from R. W. and I read each letter. I was almost in tears, because I was trying to forget him.

SENIOR YEAR

*A*t last senior year and I am looking forward to be a senior, and also looking forward to graduate. I was glad to be back at school, my last year at Marina High, then on to college to study Nursing. My dream was to be a Registered Nurse and I envisioned of going to different countries to help others.

During my senior year there was one particular teacher whom I admired for his teaching. He actually took the time and treated us with respect and there is always laughter in the class and we have so much fun. I will always remember him, he was a great Political Science teacher. I also discovered that I liked Political Science it was a very interesting subject concerning politics and governments.

Over the weekend my dad, sister's and brother and I went to the bowling Alley at the Naval Base to play a few games. To my surprise I saw my ex-boyfriend's friend and he was staring at me, my sister asked "if I knew him" then I nod my head. He came over to introduced himself to my family, and then he asked me, how I was doing? Then my dad invited him to bowl with us. After the game he asked me my phone number and if he can call me once in a while, I wrote down my phone number and hand it to him.

The next day he called and asked me out, I then told him to come for dinner and gave him direction where I live. I told mom and dad that we're having company for dinner. When Herman arrived we were playing cards and then he joined us for a game of hearts. I, then got up and went to the kitchen to help mom, and then I went to the dining room to set the dinner table.

When everything was ready and food was placed on the table, mom took the liberty to show us where to sit. During dinner everyone was talking and laughing and having a good time. I can tell Herman was enjoying his meal and feeling at ease with my family. My dad seems to like him and they have one thing in common they're both navy man.

After dinner I helped mom clean up and I can hear my dad telling my friend about the time when he was in the navy. I walked in the room and asked them if they wanted to play cards. We played a few games of poker and to make it interesting we played with poker chips.

As the night progresses and it was getting late, my parents retired for the night and also my siblings. Herman and I went to the living room to watch television. And then he told me what my ex-boyfriend said to him before he went overseas, he had asked him to watch over me while he was gone. I was surprised, and I didn't know what to say, but I did tell him that I stopped writing to him, and then he realized that I didn't want to talk about R.W.

February, Valentines Day, I went to visit Herman at the barracks and I had my sister's with me, because my dad insisted that I have to take them along. When we got there, he was waiting on me and he was surprised that I brought my sister's with me. He handed me a big valentine box with chocolate candy and a dozen roses. I really didn't expect him to get me anything for valentines day, and I felt bad because I didn't get him anything. And then we went to the bowling alley just to hang out and to get something to eat. As we were talking he mentioned that he will be on leave for two weeks to visit his family. And then he looked at me and said "we have been seeing each other for a few months, would you be my steady girl" I, then said yes, and then he handed me his class ring.

While he was gone I was busy studying for my SAT and ACT test, I was going to the library everyday after school. On Saturday morning I went to the school to take the test, and there were several students taking the test also. The SAT and the ACT test consist of multiple choices and it lasted all day and I was glad that it was over.

A week later on Monday morning, I was in my 1st period class, American Literature I was called in to the Principal's office; he then, told me the good news, that I have passed the SAT and the ACT test. When I left the principal's office I was so happy and thinking to myself which college I wanted to go to. When I went back to my class I told my girlfriends that I have passed the SAT and ACT test, they congratulated me and said "we all should go to UCLA and be roommates".

That day I got home from school and Herman was waiting on me outside my house, I was really surprised because he was to be gone for two weeks. I asked him if he had a nice visit with his family, and he replied that he did, and also he mentioned about me to his family and that they would like to meet me, I looked at him, and I didn't know what to say. I was happy to see him, but I did noticed that he has something else on his mind.

That evening we went to San Francisco and he took me to a seafood restaurant by Fisherman's Warf. It was candlelight dinner with soft music and soft lighting, I was impressed. After dinner he got out of his chair and he knelt down in front of me, and I said to him "what are you doing? Get up" then he asked me to marry him. I was stunned and surprised, I didn't know what to say, and all I noticed was some people in the restaurant was looking at us.

I sat there speechless and looking at him and thinking I'm not ready to get married, so, I told him we should go and talk about it later. When we left the restaurant we went down to the Fisherman's Warf for a walk. I, then told him that I'm not ready to get married, and that I have big plans for myself. I also told him that I wanted to go to college and go places where I have never been.

That evening he was crushed and disappointed, and I felt bad that I hurt him. I can tell that he was angry with me, then he asked me "do you even love me", then I told him "not enough to get married". Then I told him that he will find someone special to share his life with. He took me home that night and without a word from him, he drove off.

BEFORE GRADUATION

Two months before graduation, the senior student body had set a plan of activities for all the seniors before graduation:

We had our senior picnic one weekend and we had it at the park, most of everyone was there, and we all had a good time. The following weekend we had our senior pool party, and I didn't stay very long. Monday morning was the senior breakfast in the cafeteria, I remember they served us a full breakfast with pancakes, bacon, cinnamon rolls and of course breakfast drinks. The week of senior carnival day we had set up tents for games and booths for food, for the two day weekend. It was a success and we raised extra money for the senior ball. Those were the wonderful days of my senior year and it was memorable.

My best friends and I went to the mall to pick out a dress for the senior ball. And while we're in the food court I ran into Herman and invited him to sit with us, that day we started to talk again. I was glad that we can be friends again.

That night he called me just to talk. And then he would call me every night and we would talk for hours on the phone. Then, I asked him "if he would want to take me to the senior ball" he then, answered "of course, I would be honored"

I stayed home on the weekend and my dad asked about Herman; he noticed that he hasn't come to visit, and then he told me that he liked him a lot. And I told my dad that we're just friends now, and I mentioned to him, that he will be taking me to the senior ball.

I remember one day that week after school, Herman called me to meet him at the park. When I got to the park and from a distance I recognized a girl that was with him, she was one of my friends, my Filipino friend. And then I asked "what's up" and then he told me that he's been seeing my friend Donna, and that they are getting married in June. I was happy for them, I was very happy for him, that he found someone he can share his life with. And then he told me, he will still take me to the senior ball, and Donna was ok with it. I congratulated them and hugged both of them and I said "I will be there for your wedding" then I left.

SENIOR BALL

On the month of May, the day of the senior ball I went to the mall to pick up a few things that I needed for the ball. When I got home my best friend Anne was waiting for me, we had few hours before the prom, so, we listened to the music and tried different hairdo's how to style our hair for the prom.

Early evening Herman arrived at the house while I was getting ready. Anne and I entered the living room and both of our escorts had a big smile on their faces, then Herman complemented me on my dress and how beautiful I was. He handed me the flowers and then, I took one rose and pin it to his lapel, he then, took the flowers from my hands and pin it to my right shoulder.

Before the senior ball, we had a dinner reservation at the Fisherman's Warf in San Francisco at the Grotto, an Italian restaurant. The food was good, the atmosphere in the room was superb, we were enjoying each other's company, talking and laughing.

After dinner, we arrived at the Senior Ball a little late, we stopped to take pictures, and then on to our table that was reserved for us. The band, Tower of Power was playing Motown song of "I heard it through the Grapevine" everyone was on the dance floor.

I did noticed the ball room was exquisitely decorated with soft lights and party decorations, the table was decorated with beautiful flowers along with the candlelight as the centerpiece. Our theme song that night was by the Carpenters, "We've only just begun" a perfect song, everyone of us will go in different direction, a new path, and a new beginning.

After the senior ball I spent the night with Anne, we stayed up all night talking about the senior ball. I had a wonderful time, another added memory to my scrap book.

GRADUATION

On the month of June, our last month to be a senior, our classes were shortened to half a day before graduation. All the seniors were happy about the half a day class, we all had our own agenda.

A week before graduation, our senior class went through graduation exercised for four days. After practice my friends and I went to our old hang out, the hamburger place. We were talking about going to Disney Land, some of the senior's were going after graduation.

Saturday morning, the day of our graduation, three hundred and twelve students in the class of 1971, we we're all getting excited. I remember that day, the colors of the girl's cap and gown were white, and the colors of the guy's cap and gown were blue. That morning family and friends were arriving at the school campus, and everyone was taking pictures. We had our graduation ceremony outside the courtyard, it was pleasant with a little touch of the cool weather, and yet it was sunny.

Our student body president was making his speech, one thing I will always remember in his speech, when he said "that our life is going to change" and when he finished making his speech everyone stood up and gave him a big hand.

Each row was to stand up by the last letter of their last name. When it came to my row we stood up and formed a line to receive our diploma. As the Principal calls out each of our names, and when he got to me I was so happy to receive my diploma, I turned around and looked at my family with a smile, and I raised up my diploma that was in my hand.

When everyone was back at their seat, the Principal commented and said "I give you the class of 1971" and everyone stood up on their feet, and we threw our caps into the air.

After the ceremony my friends and I gathered together, hugging each other with tears in our eyes, and saying "we made it" and that particular day, I was very happy of my accomplishment.

My friends and I made an agreement that we will always be there for each other, no matter where life takes us. The four of us are the best of friends, we shared everything with each other. We laugh, we cry, we argue, but we never forget the love we have for each other.

I went home with my family after graduation to get ready to go to a wedding, my ex-boyfriend getting married to one of my Filipino friend's and on top of that my parents knows her parents, so, the whole family was invited. The wedding was beautiful, the bride and groom was so happy, and I'm glad that they found each other.

In the evening my friends and I went to a graduation party, everyone was having a good time celebrating, and some were drinking and acting foolish. We stayed for a little while, then we left. And then we went to another graduation party, we made our circle. After the rendezvous, we finally decided it's time to go home.

LIFE AFTER HIGH SCHOOL

*I*t is still the summer of 1971, I kept my job at Blue Cross and Blue shield. I stop volunteering at the hospital and decided to work five nights a week, and I was still living at home. It is the old custom of my parent's heritage, that daughter's live at home, until they get married.

One day, I told my dad that I wanted to go to college at U.C.L.A, And then he told me, that he would like for me to go to small colleges and I wouldn't have to leave home. That day I was very discontent, not the answer I wanted to hear from him.

That night as I was lying in my bed, I was soul searching. The things I wanted to do in my life seems impossible now. I was just going through the motion of every day life, but then I was thinking, going to a small college wouldn't be a bad idea. I can make the best of it, I'll be going to college during the day and working nights, and also save money while I'm still living at home.

In memory: of my father and my sister;

I will always remember the good times,

and cherished those moments we had together.

Forever in my heart.